VERONICA RUIZ MORCILLO

I am my own Prince Charming

Hope you i … lf
celebrate
this month.

Sending you lots of love!

Veronica Ruiz Morcillo
xxx

Verso Rumor.

First published by Verso Rumor 2024

First edition

This book was professionally typeset on Reedsy.
Find out more at reedsy.com

Contents

I am my own Prince Charming	v
To all of you.	vi
When I Don't Love Myself	1
Where is the now?	3
Lost on the way	5
Divine Guidance	6
My body's confession	7
We are born that woman	9
Free woman	11
My toxic relationship	13
She in me	15
Fighting to see you	17
I am failing us	19
Mesmerised by your eyes	21
My moon	22
I don't want to be a mask	24
Here you are	26
The puzzle of my life	27
At any time it's another past	28
Yesterday, Today and Tomorrow	30
This is me living	32
That before is no longer now	34
5 4 3 2 1	35
The chosen happiness	37
Chronicle of my First Date	38
By making myself vulnerable, I made us stronger.	41

Metamorphosing 42
Disney Princesses 44
Ode to my loneliness 45
Thanks, Body 47
My own desire 49
Fairy Tales 51
I take myself to be my wife 52
A Heartfelt Thank You 53

I am my own Prince Charming

By
Veronica Ruiz Morcillo

To all of you.

To my mother
To my daughters
To my sister
To my girlfriends
To my aunts
And even to my enemies…

I wish for you to recognise your light,
the one that has been hidden by centuries of imposed darkness.
I wish for you to see yourselves
with the brilliance that I now see in you,
and to finally understand
the greatness that naturally emanates from within you.

I wish for you to celebrate your
ears,
noses,
lips,
breasts,
and butts—
so imperfectly perfect
and perfectly imperfect.

I wish for you to celebrate pink
while also embracing
the entire palette of colours.

Know that there is a seat for you at the table,
even if they insist on keeping it hidden,
and that your voice is not only beautiful
but necessary,
even if they insist on ignoring it.

I wish for you to see yourselves as the goddesses you are,,
to claim the space you deserve,
and to honour one another,
rediscovering the incredible strength you already possess.

To all of you, I dedicate these *verses*.

When I Don't Love Myself

I understand now
  I don't love myself
  by forcing myself to want
  what I never truly wanted.

I understand now
  I don't love myself
  by telling you, "Yes, I'll go with you,"
  when deep down, I resist,
  or pretending, "No, it didn't hurt,"
  just to ease your mind.

I don't love myself
  by sacrificing my Saturdays
  to bury pieces of who I am,
  listening to your ego
  as it drowns in its own tears.

I don't love myself
  by spending my summer's sun
  fueling everyone else's dreams.

I don't love myself
  by hearing every voice but my own,

or finding my voice at last—
only to discover it's a whisper.

I don't love myself
by looking away from who I am,
nor by turning inward,
only to shrink from the reflection.

I don't love myself
by believing this is the only way to love.

Where is the now?

So much of life passed me by
  while I was reliving
  a yesterday that never happened.

So much of life passed me by
  while I was frozen,
  rebuilding a past no longer needed.

How much life I haven't lived
  seeking a non-existent tomorrow,
  building an illusory future.

How many hours have I turned into ashes
  while planning calendars without days,
  running after minutes,
  and abolishing months of the year?

How much of me have I buried
  by letting anguished thoughts invade me;
  annihilating sudden feelings,
  and denying the reflections of my mirrors?

How many conversations have I not listened to
  (while hearing)?

How many flavours have I not savoured
(while tasting)?
How much beauty I have not observed
(while watching)?
How much subtlety I have not felt
(while playing)?
How many experiences have I missed
(while surviving)?
How much of my life has drowned
(while breathing)?

Lost on the way

Lost on the way.
Lost, unsure of who I am.
Lost, uncertain of what I want.

I am lost inside a body
that I don't recognise.
I am lost inside thoughts
I do not understand.

Lost in countless bars
folding myself inside tequila shots.

Lost in the beds of strangers
searching for someone to guide me.

Lost in fads and theories
waiting for someone to define me.

Lost in a maze
from which only I could know the exit.

Divine Guidance

The only escape I could think of was a walk. It was the only option that avoided that suffocating situation. It was a pretence that there was life left. A walk felt the only way I could feel alive.

While wandering aimlessly across the streets of downtown, I came across a couple of strangers. I'm not much of a snooper, but it was impossible not to hear them. She told him very emphatically - *You only have two options, or survive or....*

I couldn't hear anything else. The noise and the distance diluted the sound-waves, as if fate didn't want to offer me any other options. So, I decided that this conversation was a divine sign, that there was no second choice for me, that survival was my only available alternative.

My body's confession

In the oneiric neutral ground,
my body has abandoned my soul,
as if it was a chimaera,
and transformed into another matter:
finally, she is able to look me directly.

With the exasperation of someone already fed up,
she tells me that *enough is enough*;
that it is about time
to learn how to listen to her.

She reproaches me
for so many hours wasted in:

- yoga,
- meditation,
- visualisations;

closing all my eyes
to try to 'see' her.

She shouts at me
how ironic it is
to force her into a 'personalised diet'

that ignores what she needs the most.
How fake it was
to claim my love for her
while spending hours in the gym
trying to change her.

She makes it very clear to me
how sick she is of:

- drinking water,
- eating quinoa,
- swallowing omega,
- stretching every morning
- and spending hours with useless masks on.

She yells at me, *stop fooling us.*

- A shower,
- a meal,
- exercise

has nothing to do with our legitimate self-love

Exhausted from the arguments,
my body has collapsed and confesses to me,
that the only thing she needs
is myself really looking at her in my mirror,
so I can truly love and respect her.

We are born that woman

First, we are born that woman,
we are born on a pink celluloid
of written script our future already decided/written.

We are born inside a dungeon,
masquerading as a castle,
surrounded by jailers,
who pretend to be serene
whilst reminding us
that this is where we belong.

We are born with the delusions of the other (in masculine)
with obscene fevers and impossible chills.
We are born in false monthly new bibles easily sold in any kiosks
which seduce with human freedom to ensure female submission.

We are born dressed and shod,
already thought and opined,
already lived and deceased.
We are born slaves in this feigned freedom.

We are born asleep
in a world that appears to be ours
but in which mirrors do not return our reflection.

We are born drugged,
susceptible to opiates that consensually bend us
but whose withdrawal symptoms reveal
that what was pink,
is just a veneer of a cloudy chipboard;

that our castle actually keeps us captive;

that those delusions stealthily infect our sixth senses

that those female bibles,
they corset us in women who were never born.

And then, that woman fights to be allowed to be a woman.
Fights to allow herself to be a woman.
That woman battles for our space and fights for our history,
burns palaces and plague jailers.
She is inoculated against the plague of oppression
and the evil of segregation
and screams out her own narrative
to encourage all women to really live.

Free woman

I absolutely refuse
  to be defined by your dream of femininity,
  to conform to your expectations and rules.

I steadfastly refuse
  to smile merely for vanity's sake,
  to contort my abdomen for your photographs,
  and distort it in my reflection.

I absolutely reject
  the idea of equating food with numbers,
  of adhering to false doctrines from tabloid scriptures,
  and the misappropriation of femininity.

I utterly reject
  following the false idols that appear in pixels,
  as I lie in bed watching the television.

I categorically refuse
  to listen to your interpretation of my winters,
  of my tears and downs,
  muffled by the excuse
  of your supposed 'mastery' over women snowfalls.

And I categorically refuse
  to cease my shouts, labelled as 'hysteria',
  to withhold my demands, dismissed as 'bossiness',
  to suppress my desires, branded as 'promiscuity',
  to abandon myself, accused of 'self-centeredness'.

For I am an absolute woman.
  For I am an absolute person.
  For I am unequivocally free.

My toxic relationship

I think I loved her; I am sure I loved her in the same way you read in poetry. I wanted to spend every single minute with her. I could spend hours listening to her extravagant philosophies about life and I was completely mesmerised by the crazy ideas that she only shared with me.

And I think she loved me back. I really think she loved me in the same way you see in the movies. She looked for me in every corner of our house. She begged me to stay by her side, she caught me on her breath and made me an accomplice in her life.

I really think I loved her. I loved my loneliness madly.

But despite loving her, I was ashamed of her. It was a paradox: she felt like the happiest woman in the world by her side, yet couldn't bring herself to introduce her to her closest friends.

And I really think she loved me, my loneliness loved me madly.

But despite loving me, she couldn't stop looking down on me. It was like that bully who takes advantage of your weaknesses and reminds you that she loves you *despite* you not being up to par. She keeps reminding you that she adores you, despite your hair, your body, your laughter, your crying, your life... because you are not enough, or you are too much.

The main problem was the following…. Not only did I love my loneliness and she loved me to death, but on this occasion, it really was to death. On this occasion, there was no escape, we couldn't try to forget each other, we couldn't try to shelve, to put an end to us, we couldn't send ourselves to hell. She could not report me for psychological abuse nor could I give her an ultimatum. On this occasion, a mutual agreement wasn't enough. On this occasion, the only agreement was a true reconciliation. So here I am, in an open channel, in front of humanity and in front of my particularity, working on that reconciliation, which, hopefully, will lead me to my true love.

She in me

I witness her waking up every day,
brewing coffee with her eyes sealed tight.
I trail her steps through each house nook,
where sunlight streams through windows, casting its light.

I observe her dressing up and masking her face,
applying the confidence that she struggles to find;
concealing the fragments that ache and bind.

I see her choosing her smile every morning,
smiles that are sheathed as soon as she leaves home.
smiles that I spit as soon as she gets to bed.

I watch her conceal my marks and my scuffs,
my shattered lamps and her heels worn and broken.

I see her laugh as the rain engulfs me,
I watch her breathe as the air chokes my plea.
I see her say "yes" while I cry "no" in defeat.

I watch her fighting against the tides and dragons that cheat,
while she argues with my demons, fierce and bold.

I see her continually parachuting,

with the certainty of the one who launches herself into each day,
while I fervently pray
that the parachute will open during the fall.

I witness her triumphs, even when she thinks she's failing,
even when she thinks she's just breathing.

When night descends and darkness prevails,
we merge into one, sharing the same resistance,
Intimately distant in bittersweet tears.

Only then,
from her guts (that are also my guts),
do I dare to confess that I am still here,
that I still live in her.

It is only then
that I dare to beg her:
'please don't forget about me,'
'please, trust me,'
'please look at me.'

And as I free myself from the fray,
I can finally see myself
through those familiar eyes that are also mine.

Fighting to see you

I didn't see you,
only heard the lies
whispered by guilt and spite.

I didn't love you.
I idolized an ideal,
while my expectations and false desires
were deforming you.

I didn't respect you.
I just obeyed
what I believed
would give us respect.

I didn't trust you.
I believed the whole world
except you.

I couldn't hear you
shouting,
supplicating,
to see you,
to love you,
to respect you,

to trust you.

But, in an oversight of all the demons

that deformed and silenced you,
the love of my eyes glimpsed
what was really behind you.

And, for a moment,
I could see all your love and beauty.
And, for a moment,
I could raise this temple
where at last I can see you,
bare before me,
beloved.

And here I will fight forever
to behold that love and beauty.

I am failing us

On the rare occasions,
when we are alone,
hidden under the shell of our sofa's blanket,
I observe you in our united silence
and I feel that I am failing you.

Rage and helplessness,
take over my senses
muting what I wish to shout to you.
I clench my fists
for not being enough for you.
I get angry with you
for being so elusive.

Your blindness to your beauty
infuriates me.
Your atheism, denying your magic
really pisses me off.

But what totally enrages me,
is my inability to be your guide dog,
my ineptitude to be your creed,
my incompetence to show you your divinity.

I would love to yell it at you,
tattoo it into your skin,
proclaim it to you...
But your shadows dwarf me,
making me feel insignificant,
nullifying the fact that I'm the only one
who can give meaning to our live.

Mesmerised by your eyes

While you seem to walk in your dreams,
I take advantage of your drowsiness
enchanting me with your reflection in my mirror.

I'd like to yell at you
that I love your mouth
and the mischief behind your smiles.
That I love your hands
and your sweetness which caresses my soul.
That I love your breasts
and their capacity to nurture infinite love.
And that your eyes hypnotize me,
with that childish glow
that not even wrinkles can extinguish.

But I also love your mouth
spitting out everything that hurts inside.
And I also love your hands
bleeding all the cold left by your winters.
And I also love your heart
beating uncontrollably, empowered by your fears.
And I keep being mesmerized by your eyes
burning everything in between us and the world.

My moon

I want to be the one who eats the last bit piece,
the one who gets the best piece.
I want my devotion first
and then the commitments third.

I want to invite myself to dinner on Friday,
and feel so comfortable,
that I take myself as a date to my Sunday family gathering.

I want to use my annual bonus
to take myself on trips,
so I can lose myself among infinite beaches,
and finally conquer my own land.

I want to pamper myself
treat myself to flowers,
jewels,
clothing…
I want to adore myself,
raise myself the greatest altar,
reinstate the Holy Inquisition
and exterminate any herectic
who dares to say that I am not divine.

MY MOON

I want to be my sun,
the one who warms my face
when I lean out of the window to see my spring;
the one who activates my melanin
and colours my body with love and joy.

I want to be my moon,
the one who illuminates both my darkest and most radiant nights;
the one who witnesses
my self-lust and my self-love
to melt later,
in an embrace of pure veneration.

I don't want to be a mask

Whenever you imagine big,
I don't want you to only dream.
I want you to wake up
and realize you're already living a dream.

Whenever something hurts you,
Whenever you fail
or whenever someone fails you
I don't want you to just cry
I also want you to fill your chest with pride and strength.
Pride in crying
and strength knowing
that tears always bloom in spring.

Whenever you meet a soulmate
Whenever you fell in love
I don't want you to just love.
I want you to burn,
to melt into ashes, but then rise,
knowing that with each death,
you will be a little more alive.

Whenever you look at yourself in the mirror
while getting ready to leave your sacred space

I don't want you to be ashamed of your breasts, of your hair
nor hide your cellulite under a thousand sheets.
I want you to glorify your body,
fill it with begonias
so I can water it every day
ensuring that no day passes
without having admired your perfect imperfection.

Whenever you are in the outside world
I don't want you to let your world shrink
by inherited fears, acquired or bought.
I want you to run; take flight.
I want you to ignore the borders that others have invented
and forget the limits that the anguish of your mind is dictating to you.

Don't hide behind a mask,
deform or fade into other colours.
I want you to find it easier to live
by accentuating each of your edges
and highlighting each of your pigments.

Here you are

You have arrived, with all of your luggage, just as she dreamed. You are here, after a long and arduous journey into the unknown, guided only by the wake of her longing. You are here, after being struck down and collapsing, rescued and resurrected by her ravenous desire.

But now that you're here, you seem to wish you were somewhere else. Yes, you are here, but it seems that you have forgotten why.

You have forgotten her dreams, her longings, her desires. You have forgotten that she crawled, broke, and rebuilt herself from the ashes just to bring you here. You have forgotten that that fight, that crusade, had the sole purpose of bringing you to where you are now, the place where you could be happy.

Yes, remember, she brought you here, with all her love and with all her strength. And now that you are here, it is up to you to honor and respect her. It is up to you to give life to each one of her dreams, to respond to each one of her desires, because they were also your dreams and your desires. Then, tomorrow, we will be able to look at you with as much pride and love as we now remember her. She, who was always you... and who will always be you.

The puzzle of my life

Behind that cracked window,
  at the bottom of this dim hallway,
  there are some fine drafts
  that I must have drawn in another life.

Every little death,
  every fall,
  every cry,
  has been eroding and blurring my outlines,
  twisting and transforming them,
  in asymmetric rhomboids and curvilinear lines
  that fit harmoniously
  in this puzzle of my life.

At any time it's another past

Suddenly, I'm here again.
  Suddenly, the years have not passed (10 years),
  Suddenly, I'm not a mother,
  not in a couple,
  nor an employee,
  nor an expatriate.

Suddenly, I'm back in my cave,
  in my house,
  in my bed.

Suddenly, I am reborn, waiting.

Waiting
  to hear my sister's voice from her room.

Waiting
  for my father to open the front door.

Waiting
  for my mother to pick up the ringing phone.

It feels like another life,
  another story,

another family.

A sister who is now another sister.
A father who is now another father.
A mother who is now another mother.

A life that no longer exists.
A finished story.
A metamorphosed family.

My adolescent shadow looks at me from my sheets
with tears in its eyes
Then, the reflection of my future body
cradles me, knowing how to lull the past
back into the present
in a passionate kiss.

Yesterday, Today and Tomorrow

Every fall,
  every shame,
  every mistake,
  every fight,
  every pain.

Every word out of place,
  every moment that you lived,
  every fight you fought,
  and every tear you shed...

I want you to know that it was not in vain,
  my love.

I want you to know
  that my today
  has evolved from each bullet
  and from every tear.
  I want you to know
  that my tomorrow
  thanks you for each stumble
  and for every torment.

I want you to know

that from here,
in this limbo of space and time,
everything translates into
your great vitality
and your eternal smile.

This is me living

My stumbling feet, both block and guide,
for I am the one who falls and rises high.
Each tumble is a step towards the next stride,
this is me, discovering as I try.

My hands, sometimes clumsy and inept,
are also the ones that bring flourish, adept.
Each challenge is an opportunity to accept,
this is me growing, with each skill kept.

My body, a vessel, ever untried,
I'm the fresh-faced initiate, the seasoned guide.
Every encounter, subject, or unknown terrain,
is a reminder that beginnings shall ever remain.
This is me, learning, adapting with might,
embracing the challenges that come into sight.

My lips, at times, bear words of offense,
yet I'm the seeker of pardon, a voice in defence.
Every spoken wound, a blind fury's toll,
every glimpse of regret unveils my soul.
For, in assimilation, I strive to be whole,
this is me, growing, becoming bold.

My skin, with scars etched deep and wide,
is also the canvas where beauty resides.
Each wound seals my strength inside,
each scar etched is a testament to what I've been,
shaping the beauty of my soul,
because this is me, living, embracing life's fray.

That before is no longer now

The silence that used to scare me
is now the voice that I seek;
it is the sweet whisper that soothes me.

Those imposed withdrawals in which I was previously imprisoned
are now the oases to which I escape;
a sofa and warm blanket, book in hand, on a winter Sunday.

This loneliness that used to embarrass me
is now a best friend who takes care of me;
a companion of wanderings and feats.

The shame which I used to hide
is now the pride of my accents,
which guide through the rest of my canvas.

This introversion that I didn't understand before
is now what best explains my most intimate self
and which gives meaning to my most coveted desires.

Those *before qualities,*
previously misunderstood and marginalised,
are now
the honour and glory of my current *now.*

5 4 3 2 1

Bringing our attention to our senses anchors us in the present and counting the elements interrupts the spin of our thoughts. (Ellen Hendricksen).

'I'm here.
I am present.'

I see the field around me,
the highway that crosses my house,
the birds that play,
the clouds disperse,
and the steps that I'm taking.

I hear the cars driving away,
a plane over my head,
the chirping of the sparrows that sing to me,
and a dog that barks at them.

I feel the wind on my face,
the stones against my shoes,
the cotton on my skin.

I smell the spice mix from the Indian restaurant on this sidewalk,
the vetiver perfume of the man who overtakes me.

I taste this coffee that keeps me awake.

I see my smallness in this immense greatness.
I hear the whispers of nature.
I feel the love of this land.
I smell the pollution that torments us.
I taste the thirst of life.

I'm here.
I am present.

The chosen happiness

It doesn't matter what dreams I throw away. It wouldn't even matter if I didn't have you by my side. Because, in all the ways, in all those lives lived and not lived, I could be equally as happy or just as unhappy as I am at this moment, in this life, in this fragment of my story.

Chronicle of my First Date

'It is time to give myself a chance,' I thought. 'If I have given opportunities to the weirdest guys on dating apps, attending predictably horrible first dates, why do I keep avoiding setting up a date with myself?' I grabbed the phone and made a reservation at one of my favourite restaurants. 'First step is done,' I said to myself and marked the date in bold in my calendar.

The day in question came too quickly. I woke up excited and anguished. The idea of spending an entire evening with myself was terrifying. What would happen if I didn't like myself? What would I do if we ran out of conversation topics? How would I break those awkward silences without making things even more awkward?

Perhaps I needed a plan b, an escape, a random party to take myself, so strangers could solve the potential scenario of not knowing what to do with myself.

But that would be too easy, at the slightest hesitation I would have ended up at that party and this date would have been another of my failures. So, I discarded plan b and decided to go all for it. 'After all, I'm sure I have dealt with worse situations,' I comforted myself.

I bought myself some flowers and took one of my treat showers; shaved as if I expected to have the best sex of my entire life and used the perfume for special occasions. I looked for my best lingerie at the bottom of the drawer and put on one of those dresses that make me feel that I am a goddess on Earth.

I left home on autopilot. I focused on looking for a taxi. I got to the restaurant and slowly walked towards my table, with my stomach dominated by nervousness instead of appetite. I sat down and ordered a dry martini. The first sip whispered that the first step had already been taken, I was already there, I was already in front of myself, and 'damn, she looks hot and seems nice'.

Conversation began as these conversations usually begin, with a, 'what do you do for a living?' and,'How do you spend your free time?' I tried to go quickly through those topics, I didn't want to dive too much. I didn't want to unveil the frustrations of broken dreams or dormant ambitions; I didn't want to confess that in my free time I felt more 'slave' than 'free'. But I must have been very good at asking questions, and even better at reading between lines and looks because, after mourning my losses, we began to glimpse my triumphs. And after glimpses of my triumphs, we began to build my hopes. By the time we ordered dessert, I felt that I knew myself so much that not only I could name my traumas by their nicknames, but I could also draw every inch of my soul.

The more I knew, the more I understood myself. The more I understood myself, the more I believed that I could love this face that smiled and cried in equal parts. I was falling in love and I could see a ' happily ever after'.

We finished dinner and paid (shared) the bill. I was definitely taking myself to have the last one at home, where there would be no distractions, and where I could get completely naked. I wanted to kiss me, hold me, and give me all the love I had denied myself for many years.

I uncorked my best bottle of wine and we let each sip heal a wound, until there were no cuts to heal or victories to celebrate, just a naked body whose time it had come to honour. I took out my best toys and savoured myself like never before, I made love to myself like no one had ever done.

The morning woke us up with a smile on my face, hugging myself, with the spring blossing in my stomach; 'I have finally found the one' I thought, 'I had finally found me'.

By making myself vulnerable, I made us stronger.

By making myself vulnerable, I made us stronger.
By making myself vulnerable, I healed from my past.
By making myself vulnerable, I resurrected my future self.

Metamorphosing

I have shed my skin many times,
  and changed in shape on so many occasions.

I have gone from egg to larva
  without knowing very much
  about how not to stay alone in my chrysalis.
  I have been a tadpole and I have been a frog.
  I have been a person and I have been a cockroach.

I have tried to be a man
  and I have tried to be a woman.
  I have wanted to dance, to rock and roll
  fully dressed like a mod.
  I have prayed to all the creeds
  and I have joined in the burning of churches and temples.
  I have pretended to be high class
  and I have raised my proletarian fist.
  I have been an idealist
  and I have embraced existentialist nausea.
  I have daydreamed
  and I have dreamt while sleeping.
  I have tried to be of pure creation
  and I have fought to be an empire.

At each stage and every attempt,
a part of me has died,
leaving behind ashes
that my resurrection collects.

I felt brave enough one day
to peek and have a look at my reflection
And *Oh My God*
I was amazed when I saw
Such a goddess in a butterfly conformation.

A sooty butterfly
of male and female,
of gold and zinc,
of fervour and earthiness.
A butterfly smudged
with bright pigments
of wild sweetness,
A goddess empowered by her dreams,
A goddess reigning over her conquered being.

Disney Princesses

I am the kiss that wakes me up,
  the lips that save me,
  the prince who finds my shoe,
  the warrior who fights against the villains.

I am my enchanted beast,
  the one who saves me from dubious wolves
  and arrogant 'Gaston's.

I am the seven protective dwarfs,
  I'm Sebastian, Mushu, Lumiere.
  I am the genie of my own lamp,
  my fierce guardian Rajah.

I am my prince and my princess.
  I am my moral.
  I relate to you my beginning,
  and I reveal to myself my own end.

Ode to my loneliness

How not to love my precious solitude,
courting me with imagination,
charming me with her curiosity;
seducing me with whispers of common projects
and fascinating me by recreating our desires?

How not to love my beloved loneliness,
if my loneliness has led me
to other space-time planes?
My loneliness has given me a vital breeze,
and it has kidnapped me
to follow my dreams.

My loneliness has been my forbidden love.
It has been my dog in the manger.
It has been the one that always came back
after too many mouths
and too many tequilas
at five in the morning.

My loneliness has been my breath.
It has been my fuel.
It has been my shelter.

So,
how not to love my prince forever,
and my most fervent lover?
How not to love my friend for life,
and my most loyal guide?

Loneliness,
always yours,
always mine,
always ours.

Thanks, Body

Naked,
staring at the mirror-image of this body that supports me,
I can only cheer a huge *thank you*
while I let myself be fascinated
by all the folds
of its continuous transformations.

Thank you for forgiving me
for so many misdeeds and negligence.
Thank you for forgetting
so much abuse and unkindness.

Thank you for holding me up
even when I was fading.
Thank you for keeping me walking
even when tiredness tried to convince me
that it was all in vain.

Thank you for your peachy skin
that welcomes each scar
and turns them into beautiful engravings of my history.

Thank you for this thorough river system
that navigates through my veins,

ensuring the quenching
of each of my desires.

Thank you for these euphoric hands
that guide, create and shape my paths
while caressing and touching the lives of others.

Thank you for these blooming breasts
which can brim with passion,
that can create and feed,
that can soothe and protect.

Thank you for these erectile pegs,
providers of hours of love and ecstasy,
confirming the naturalness of my delusions and outbursts.

Thank you for these monthly bacchanalias,
authentic covens of hormones
that seduce and trick me
down an unknown path,
through all my layers.

Thank you for this changing womb,
pure alchemy, capable of creating life,
and for this brain, continuously boiling,
and the ability of choice.

Thank you for my gut-instinct,
that gives tongue to my stomach
and the strength to flee from wars and embrace concords.

Thank you, glorious body.
Thank you, miraculous body.

My own desire

It's like a ritual:
myself in my own loving nest.
I wait for everything to calm down,
and silence to settle.

I light a couple of scented candles
in the darkness of my space.
Dim light, and enveloping fragrance,
recreates an atmosphere
in which to feel attractive.

I begin by
unbuttoning
slowly
my blouse,
while I go
sliding
down
little
by
little
my panties.

Slowly,
no hurry.

My naked shadow is starting to get excited.

Both of my hands know where to go.

The shrewd right rushes to my hips,
drawing eager circles around my angles.
The restless left plays with the gap between my breasts,
skirting to the tip of my erect breasts.

The rhythmic sound of my breathing
is leading the compass of my fingers.
An allegro start
so I can recreate myself
in each one of my recesses.
Then it speeds up,
looking to shake my whole body.

Masturbation,
onanism,
self-love for tonight.
A night in which I love myself.
A night in which I honour myself.
A night in which I am
my own desire.

Fairy Tales

I looked for you in every pair of lips I kissed.
I looked for you in every hug, every smile,
each friendly face I met.
I cried for you with each of my unjustified tears.
I loved you in each person I didn't hold dear.
I felt you in every rhythm
that danced with my being.
I felt you in each verse
that whispered that you exist.
I chased you across cities and oceans,
forests and heavens.
I chased you across thousands of pages,
infinite endpoints and letters.

One day, you just appeared,
leaning out from the reflection of my mirror
you kissed our dormant lips,
slid the glass slipper onto our foot.
Our heart finally found peace
and I all lived happily ever after.

I take myself to be my wife

My love,
I want you to know
that it won't be easy,
that there will be difficult times,
that there will be days when I want to abandon myself
and hours when I want to hate myself.

But I also know,
from the depths of each of my pores,
that I want to learn to love myself
every day of my life.

Thus –
I take myself to be my wife
I promise to be true to myself,
in good times and in bad,
in sickness and in health,
and I will love me
and honor me
all the days of my life.

Always me, forever.

A Heartfelt Thank You

Thank you for joining me on this journey through words. I hope these poems have resonated with you, empowered you, and reminded you of your own light and strength. Your support means the world to me, and I would love to hear what you thought of the book. If you enjoyed it, please consider leaving a review on Amazon — your feedback helps others discover this book.

You're also invited to visit my website - versorumor.com, where you'll find some specially designed merchandise inspired by this book. If you have something in mind that isn't available, feel free to email me—I'd be happy to create something just for you! As a thank you for your support, use the code **POETRY10** for a 10% discount on your next purchase.

Thank you again for being part of this journey. Your voice, your light, and your presence are powerful. See you in the next book!

Printed in Great Britain
by Amazon

56866590R00036